Florida-Backroads-Travel.com

FLORIDA
EVERGLADES

Second Edition, 2017

CONTENTS

INTRODUCTION

Florida Everglades is a short book whose mission is to teach you a bit about the history of the Everglades and what is being done currently to try to save and restore this great natural resource. The book will take you on a trip through the ancient and modern history of this unique place. Much of the material in this book comes from the website **Florida-Backroads-Travel.com**.

There are dozens of governmental and nongovernmental organizations whose sole reason to exist is the preservation of the Everglades. Sometimes these entities all seem to be on the same page. In other cases they seem to disagree among each other about what is best for this delicate place that man has so negatively impacted.

This book is organized into six separate periods of history and discusses each in brief detail. It is my hope that this small book will add a little clarity to the problem and help you understand some of the issues.

OVERVIEW OF THE EVERGLADES

The map below of South Florida shows the boundaries of the Everglades and the locations of features that influence the environment. The area of influence extends north to Orlando and west to Cape Coral, Naples and Key West.

This map is courtesy of Wikipedia.

The Florida Everglades is a huge subtropical wetland of sawgrass marshes in a complex system of interdependent ecosystems. These ecosystems include cypress swamps, the estuarine mangrove forests of the Ten Thousand Islands, tropical hardwood hammocks, pine rock land, and the salt water marine environment of Florida Bay in the Keys.

The western parts of the extremely urban southeast Florida counties of Martin, Palm Beach, Broward and Miami-Dade are in the Everglades. The rampant development in this megalopolis has created new problems for the Everglades and aggravated old ones.

Also, although Naples, Fort Myers, Labelle, Immokalee and Everglades City are in southwest Florida, the Everglades ecosystem touches their very back doors and is part of their history and future.

The Florida Everglades sprawls across 16 counties, all the way from Orlando in the north to Monroe County in the south. It was the last region of Florida to see significant development, but when it did it happened with a vengeance.

The centerpiece of the Everglades is shallow **Lake Okeechobee**, second in size only to Lake Michigan in the list of largest freshwater lakes completely within the boundaries of the 48 continental United States.

Historically, the areas north of Lake Okeechobee drained into the lake via natural waterways including the **Kissimmee River**. When the water levels in Lake Okeechobee built up, the overflows traveled slowly south through the marshes and

3

sloughs to **Florida Bay**, the salt water body that separates mainland Florida from the Keys.

This area south of Lake Okeechobee, about 60 miles wide and 100 miles deep, was coined **The River of Grass** by **Marjory Stoneman Douglas** in her book of the same name. This sheet flow moved slowly south at the average speed of about **one half mile per day**. Sometimes it would take two summer rainy seasons before the water would make it to Florida Bay.

This long journey was essential to the balance of the Everglades ecology, and to the purification of storm water before it soaked back into the ground or found its way to the bay. Most of south Florida relies on the Everglades and its recharged water for their drinking water supply.

The sections of this book that follow will show you how this natural system has been altered.

ANCIENT HISTORY: 13,000 BC to 1817

Native American Period: 13,000 BC to 1565

Humans were living in the Florida Everglades area as long as 15,000 years ago. Two major tribes - the **Calusa** and the **Tequesta** - lived as hunter-gatherers on the edges of the rich Florida Everglades ecosystems.

There may have been about 4,000 to 7,000 Calusa at their peak. The Tequesta were much smaller in number and occupied a smaller territory. The Calusa were the largest and most powerful tribe in Florida, and lived in 50 settlements from Lake Okeechobee to the Gulf in Southwest Florida and the Florida Keys.

The Tequesta lived in several small settlements in Southeast Florida including one at the mouth of the **Miami River** at Biscayne Bay.

These Native Americans were hunter gatherers, and lived off seafood from the Gulf of Mexico and the Atlantic Ocean, and animals and plants from the nearby Florida Everglades.

The Tequesta and Calusa have disappeared from Florida.

Spanish and British Period: 1565 to 1817

The Spaniards settled Pensacola in 1559 and St Augustine in 1565, and owned Florida for most of the next 256 years until Florida became a U.S. territory in 1821, with a brief period of British ownership from 1763-1784.

During their ownership, the Spaniards and British didn't pay much attention to the Florida Everglades. They considered it a god forsaken worthless land full of miserable animals and a few insignificant Indians.

The Everglades were first mentioned in writing on Spanish maps made by map makers who had never seen the land. Their name for this mysterious area between the Atlantic Ocean and the Gulf of Mexico was **"Laguna del Espiritu Santo"**, which means **"Lake of the Holy Spirit"**.

The Spaniards had limited contact with the Calusa and Tequesta who lived on the outer fringes of the Florida Everglades at the mouths of rivers and streams and coastal ridges and hammocks.

Like most indigenous populations in the Americas, the Indians in Florida did not prosper under Spanish rule. The Indian populations began to decline until by the mid 1700s most of them were gone.

The Seminoles, a tribe of Creeks who assimilated other peoples - including escaped slaves - into their own, were slowly forced into migrating to Florida by development in the Carolinas and Georgia.

The Seminoles made their living in North and Central Florida until later years when they were squeezed into the Florida Everglades by the U.S. military in the Seminole Wars.

SEMINOLE WARS: 1817 to 1858

The Florida Everglades had a turbulent and violent history in the years from 1817 to 1881.

Spain still owned Florida in 1817, but the U.S. government was fighting Indians who were feuding with American settlers in Florida and south Georgia. The First Seminole War was from 1817 to 1818. The United States acquired Florida from Spain in 1821, and it became a territory. Florida became a state in 1845.

Not much was happening in the Everglades when Florida became a state. The remote region had almost no settlement, agriculture, development or industry.

As white settlers began to move into North and Central Florida, conflicts and violence between them and the Seminole Indians became a problem that the government tried to solve by moving the Seminoles to western reservations.

The Indians didn't always want to move, so three **Seminole Wars** took place on Florida soil.

First Seminole War: 1817 to 1818.

Second Seminole War: 1835 to 1842.

Third Seminole War: 1855 to 1858.

These wars saw most of the Seminoles either killed or transplanted to reservations in the western United States. The Seminoles never surrendered, and those that survived escaped into the Florida Everglades where their descendants still live.

Many Florida place names date back to the old primitive fortifications of the Seminole Wars.

Some of these include:

> Fort Lauderdale
> Fort Pierce
> Fort Myers
> Fort Drum
> Fort Ogden
> Fort Meade
> Fort Brooke (Tampa)
> Fort King (Ocala)
> Fort Basinger.

Many other Florida place names come from Seminole leaders and the places that the Seminoles called home.

The town of **Micanopy** near Gainesville was named in honor of the great war chief of the Second Seminole War. The name is pronounced **MICK-UH-NOPIE** that rhymes with Opie, Sheriff Andy's son in the old television program **The Andy Griffith Show**.

That is **Chief Micanopy** in the portrait above.

Another great leader in the Second Seminole War was **Osceola**. Even though not a tribal chief, he had great influence with Micanopy and the other Seminoles.

Osceola was born **Billy Powell** in 1804 in Alabama. Billy was apparently a mix of Native American, English, Irish, Scottish and African American. He was a one man United Nations, and his heritage may have helped him become such a great leader.

Many surnames of Seminole origin still survive in the areas around the Florida Everglades. Some typical ones include **Osceola**, **Billie** and **Bowlegs**.

The Seminoles are the only Indian nation never to sign a peace treaty with the U.S.

Their legacy of never surrendering is proudly carried on by the **Florida State Seminole** athletic program. One of the greatest of all college football traditions takes place at home games in **Doak Campbell Stadium** in Tallahassee.

A student portraying Osceola charges down the field riding an Appaloosa war horse named **Renegade** and plants a flaming spear at midfield to begin every home game.

Even this old Gator fan admits to loving the spectacle.

That is Osceola in the portrait above.

The U.S. Civil War took place from 1861 to 1865, and Florida was a Southern state whose role was mainly providing food and other agricultural products to the battling Confederate armies further north.

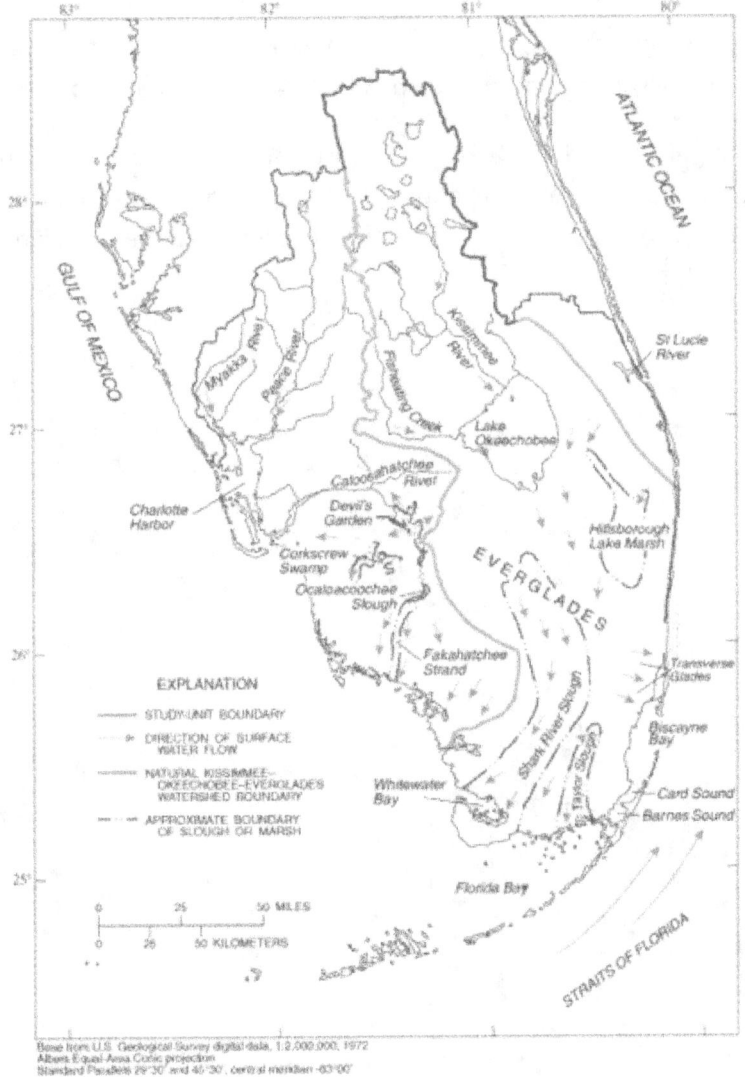

The State was consumed by the War and the painful Reconstruction period that followed until **1877**. The Florida

Everglades remained pretty much as it had for thousands of years except for the Seminole Indians who lived off the land and waters.

The waters continued to flow in the Everglades as they had historically done and as shown on the Wikipedia map above.

The historic flow that had nurtured the Everglades for thousands of years was about to change. Florida was about to enter into several economic booms that featured the Everglades as a star player.

RECLAMATION & AGRICULTURE: 1881 to 1930

Reclamation and agricultural development were the focus in the years from 1881 to 1930. This period in Everglades history was all about **"drain, baby, drain!"**

In 1881 Florida was still suffering from the economic ravages of the **Civil War** and the **Reconstruction** years that followed. Florida, along with other states of the old **Confederacy**, was just about broke.

The State was looking for ways to raise money for its routine operations, and for ways to encourage development and agriculture and increase its tax base. The State saw an answer in the millions of acres of **"worthless"** swampland it owned in the Everglades and in other undeveloped properties it owned on the west coast of Florida.

In those days, most people felt that a swamp was just a useless piece of real estate that had no value until it was drained, developed and cultivated.

In 1881, the State sold 4,000,000 acres - an area larger than Connecticut - to a northern industrialist named **Hamilton Disston**. He paid 25 cents per acre, and it was apparently the largest land purchase by any single person in the history of the world.

Disston tried very hard to drain the northern Florida Everglades south of Orlando and north of Lake Okeechobee. He piled a fortune on top of his million dollar land purchase price. He built canals and dredged rivers and opened the interior of central Florida to steamboat navigation.

13

He dredged the meandering **Kissimmee River** south to Lake Okeechobee. He then connected the big lake to the Caloosahatchee River so that steamboats could make the trip from **Fort Myers** to **Kissimmee**. Central Florida was now connected to the world via the **Gulf of Mexico**.

Disston's efforts started the first land boom in Florida history. He was responsible for creating or growing **Kissimmee** and **St. Cloud** in Central Florida, and **Gulfport**, **Tarpon Springs** and **St. Petersburg** in Central West Florida.

He also started the successful growing and harvesting of rice and sugar cane near Kissimmee. Most of the drainage systems installed by Disston almost 130 years ago are still functioning today in the Kissimmee and St. Cloud areas.

All of these efforts to drain the Everglades, however, fell short. He was unable to significantly lower the surface water around **Lake Okeechobee** and in the Everglades, but his activities were the beginning of development and agriculture in the area.

His achievements made it possible for **Henry Flagler** to build his railroad down the east coast of Florida, and for **Henry Plant** to build his railroad to the west coast at Tampa. The two railroads and their hotels were the beginning of Florida's tourism and agriculture industries.

Another important figure in the reclamation period was **Richard J. "Dicky" Bolles**. In 1908, the State of Florida sold him 500,000 acres in the Everglades for $2 an acre. As part of the purchase, the State promised to spend half the sale proceeds for drainage and reclamation.

Bolles founded the **Florida Fruit Lands Company** to sell 180,000 acres in Dade and Palm Beach Counties. The company subdivided the land into 12,000 individual farm sites of various sizes and designated a site for a new town named **"Progreso."** They had plans for streets, factories, schools, churches and infrastructure.

This created another of Florida's famous land booms. For $240, buyers could purchase the right to bid on a farm and town lot through a scheduled auction. He also used the same sales technique to sell his remaining 420,000 acres through another company of his, **Okeechobee Fruit Lands Company**.

His salesmen fanned out throughout the country promoting the Everglades as a **"Garden of Eden,"** a **"Tropical Paradise"** and a **"Promised Land."** His promotions even had the endorsement of State and Federal officials who touted the fertility of the Everglades land.

Bolles's deals began to fall apart by 1911. He held a giant auction in Fort Lauderdale, and it was only then that holders of the $240 options found out there would be no genuine auction. Instead, they were required to buy land that had been picked out for them. Most of the land was still under water.

There were huge lawsuits, and the court let Bolles keep the deposits but wouldn't let him sell any land until the State had done its part in draining the Everglades.

Bolles was arrested in 1913 but was found innocent. He maintained that he believed what State and Federal officials had told him about the Everglades, and that he was only acting on that information.

Bolles died in 1917, and along with him the dreams of his Everglades land buyers. There is no town of Progreso, the land contracts expired and most of the land Bolles sold went back to the State for nonpayment.

FLOOD CONTROL: 1930 to 1971

The Florida Everglades grew in population as a result of the drainage improvements completed from 1881 to 1928. Many new communities were formed in the vicinity of the Everglades in those years.

Two of the worst hurricanes in Florida history stormed ashore in 1926 and 1928 and caused Lake Okeechobee to burst through its levees, drowning thousands of people. The 1928 disaster was the worst in Florida hurricane history.

The Federal and State governments began to concentrate now on flood control rather than drainage. The **Okeechobee Flood Control District** was created in 1929.

Between 1930 and 1937, the U.S. Army Corps of Engineers built a 66 mile long dike around the southern edge of Lake Okeechobee. The 20 foot high embankment was named for **President Herbert Hoover**. The Corps also set the legal limits of surface water elevation on the lake between **14 and 17** feet above sea level.

At the same time, an 80 foot wide 6 foot deep canal was built along the winding path of the narrow upper Caloosahatchee River. Whenever the lake levels got too high, the excess water was released through the canal and went on down to the Gulf of Mexico. This project was part of the 1937 completion of the **Okeechobee Waterway**. Sugar cane production soared after these flood control improvements, and the populations of the small towns around the lake tripled by the end of World War Two.

As soon as the Hoover dike was completed, however, people began to notice detrimental effects in the Everglades.

An extended drought in the late 1930s highlighted the problem. The Hoover dike prevented water from leaving the lake into the surrounding lands by sheet flow. The peaty soils dried up and turned into dust. Salty water from the ocean intruded into Miami's wells because the Everglades water wasn't getting there.

In 1939 a million acres of Everglades burned and the black clouds of soot from the peat and sawgrass fires made it difficult to breathe in Miami.

The low ground water levels caused the peaty soils to shrink and subside and many homes around Lake Okeechobee had to be put on stilts and raised up as much as 8 feet to get back to the elevations that their homes were before the dike was built.

More hurricanes in 1947 caused severe flooding, and the **Central and Southern Florida Flood Control Project** (C&SF) was formed to construct flood control improvements in the Everglades.

About this same time, Everglades National Park was officially dedicated in 1947. It was a good thing for the long term protection of the Everglades, but to understand the impact on some of the local residents read books about that period. An example of one such book is "**Totch: A Life in the Everglades**" by Loren G. Brown.

The C&SF built 1,400 miles of canals, numerous flood gates and pump stations and levees up until 1971. The final project was the 22 miles long C-38 canal, which straightened the natural meandering course of the Kissimmee River on its way to Lake Okeechobee.

The C-38 project almost immediately started causing serious damage to animal and plant communities and negatively impacted the water quality in the region.

RESTORATION: 1971 to 2000

The focus in the 1970s became how to undo what man has done. The Florida Everglades was being destroyed by all of the drainage, development activity and agricultural fertilizer and wastewater runoff. It became horrifyingly evident to thoughtful Americans that something drastic had to be done.

The issue came to a head in the early 1970s. **Miami International Airport** was jammed up with traffic and didn't have much room for expansion in its urban Miami location. A proposal was submitted to construct a huge jetport in the **Big Cypress Swamp**.

Studies soon showed that the jetport would destroy the South Florida ecosystem and Everglades National Park. Local governments, environmentalists, other activists and even nationally prominent politicians mobilized intense opposition to the project.

From this pivotal event, local, state and federal governments began to cooperate in finding ways to balance the needs of urban and agricultural Florida with the Everglades natural environment.

The **C-38 Canal (Kissimmee River)** became the first C&SF project to be restored. In the 1980s, the government began to backfill the canal. In many cases they used the original soils excavated from the river. The restoration of the Kissimmee River is scheduled to be completed in 2019.

In 1986 high levels of phosphorous and mercury were discovered in the Everglades waterways after years of fertilizer runoff from agricultural operations. Now Florida Everglades water quality quickly became a focus.

Many legal battles were fought between various governments to decide who was responsible for monitoring and enforcing water quality standards. Finally, in 1994, the **Everglades Forever Act** was passed. Since then the **South Florida Water Management District (SFWMD)** and the **U.S. Army Corps of Engineers** have cooperated in programs that have greatly reduced phosphorous levels.

Other government and private studies, however, showed that the quality of life in South Florida was in decline and that the region could not sustain its growth.

The studies predicted serious environmental decline, water shortages and a devastated tourist economy.

COMPREHENSIVE EVERGLADES RESTORATION PLAN: 2000 to ?

Finally, in 2000, after years of study and legal battles, a strategy called the Comprehensive Everglades Restoration Plan (CERP) was passed into law to restore portions of the Everglades, Lake Okeechobee, the Caloosahatchee River and Florida Bay. CERP is a joint venture of the Federal and State governments, and is managed by the U.S. Army Corps of Engineers and the South Florida Water Management District.

It was originally estimated that the over 60 major projects that comprise CERP would take 30 years to complete and cost about $8 billion. Like most complex government projects, those estimates are being continually updated.

The objective of CERP is to restore as much as possible of the original water flows that historically made the Everglades the treasure it was. The plan also has to provide flood protection for people and property. It's a difficult balancing act that has all kinds of political ramifications along with economic and environmental impacts.

Everybody fervently hopes that CERP will go a long way toward reversing the decline of the Everglades that has been taking place since Hamilton Disston first started his drainage projects almost 130 years ago.

The complicated provisions of CERP are beyond the scope of this little book. More information is available in this book by referencing the links on page 50.

SOME EVERGLADES TOWNS and PLACES

Many Florida towns and cities are influenced by Lake Okeechobee and the Everglades. This influence is felt by towns not just in the Everglades, but along the southeast and southwest coasts of Florida. These towns, if not quite in the Everglades, are close to it, affect it and are affected by it.

A low ridge separates the Everglades from the Atlantic Ocean, and the areas between the ocean and the ridge were developed first. Henry Flagler built his Florida East Coast Railway along this ridge. As the areas grew in population, they sprawled west into the Everglades.

Many southeast Florida towns have had their western suburbs carved out of the Florida Everglades. West Palm Beach, Fort Lauderdale and Miami are notable examples along with most of the towns in between.

The southwest Florida coast developed later than the southeast because there was no easy way to cross the Everglades from southeast Florida to Naples and Fort Myers. The Tamiami Trail, completed in 1928, opened up southwest Florida to development.

Towns that didn't exist or only started growing when the Everglades were drained include:

Belle Glade, Canal Point, Clewiston, Everglades City, Lakeport, Moore Haven, Okeechobee, Pahokee, Port Mayaca, St. Cloud and South Bay.

Things to Do In the Florida Everglades Towns

There are many things to do in the Florida Everglades towns including ecotourism, fishing, gambling at the Indian casinos, airboat rides, watching alligator wrestling and a host of other activities. Lodging and restaurants are also available at most of the towns in the Everglades area.

The **Okeechobee Waterway** provides one of the most interesting side trips in this part of the country. You can enjoy it by boat or at the several recreational areas adjacent to the locks and dams along the route.

A famous resident of the Loop Road back in the day was **Ervin Rouse**, the composer of **"The Orange Blossom Special."** He never made much money from this song and used to play for drinks at the old Gator Hook Lodge on Big Cypress Loop Road.

Another interesting side trip is to take Big Cypress Loop Road south of Tamiami Trail between Naples and Miami and visit Lucky Cole's place.

Lucky Cole is a well-known Everglades photographer who specializes in nude photos of women in tropical settings. He is not to be confused with another well-known Everglades photographer, **Clyde Butcher**.

They are both talented photographers but specialize in different forms of natural beauty.

This photograph is courtesy of Lucky Cole.

Everglades City

Everglades City is on the Barron River south of Tamiami Trail in Collier County. It is at the end of State Road 29 and takes about 35 minutes to drive there from downtown Naples. The population is around 600 people, more or less.

Everglades City is a convenient place to stay while exploring the Everglades, Chokoloskee Island and the 10,000 islands. It is a place of magic and mystery. It is also a place where hardworking Florida Crackers eked out a living from the shallow waters of the mangrove fringed Everglades.

Charlton Tebeau wrote a classic book, **"The Story of the Chokoloskee Bay Country,"** that tells about the history of the entire area.

A longtime resident of Chokoloskee Island, the late Totch Brown wrote **"Totch: A Life in the Everglades"** that has the authentic flavor of somebody who was born and raised there.

Long before Totch's ancestors came to the Chokoloskee Bay country, the Calusa Indians lived in the area. Early settlers said that the Indians grew potatoes along the banks of the Barron River.

The first white settlers began to show up after the Civil War.

The first permanent settler was **William Smith Allen** who came to the area in 1873. Another early pioneer was **George W. Storter, Jr.**, who raised sugar cane.

Storter also opened a trading post and post office, and began to entertain Yankee tourists who came to Everglades City on their yachts to hunt and fish.

His house eventually became the **Everglades Road and Gun Club**. It has been visited by many famous people, including U.S. presidents.

The entire Chokoloskee Bay area, Marco Island and Naples were in Lee County in those days. Barron Collier, a successful Memphis businessman, came to the area in 1922 and bought thousands of acres.

In 1923 the Florida Legislature created Collier County from Lee County, and Everglades City became the county seat. It was first named Everglade, then Everglades, and finally Everglades City.

Collier pushed the completion of the **Tamiami Trail (US-41)** from Naples to Miami, and in 1929 built State Road 29 south to Everglades City.

It was the first time the little town had ever been connected to the rest of Florida by road.

Hurricane Donna visited southwest Florida in 1960 and left tremendous damage in its wake. Everglades City was especially hard hit.

After Hurricane Donna, the County seat was moved from Everglades City to East Naples, where it still is today.

Everglades City was once known as the **"The Square Grouper Capital."** In the 1970s and 1980s, Everglades City and Chokoloskee became notorious for their trade in "square grouper," a euphemism for bales of marijuana. Boats and airplanes were dropping the stuff into the mangroves of the 10,000 islands where it was picked up by locals and delivered all over the United States.

During Ronald Reagan's **"War on Drugs"** most of the activity was stopped and had completely dried up by the end of the 1980s.

Everglades City has a couple of interesting historic buildings: The Rod and Gun Club and the old Collier County Courthouse along with several weathered cottages.

Moore Haven

Moore Haven is a small town of about 1700 people located on the southwest shoreline of Lake Okeechobee. Although it is the county seat of **Glades County**, it is a sleepy little town that is on the western edge of the Everglades agricultural area. When you drive through it seems to be a poor town with not much going for it, but its location at the junction of the Caloosahatchee River canal and Lake Okeechobee give it some potential.

The site of Moore Haven was first occupied by early Native Americans, and later Seminoles.

The town was named after its founder, James A. Moore. In its early days, Moore Haven was often called **"Little Chicago"** because it was located at the junction of the Caloosahatchee River Canal and Lake Okeechobee which reminded people of

31

Chicago's fortunate position at the southern end of Lake Michigan.

It was a significant boom town in the days when riverboats came past Moore Haven with their cargos of cattle, fruit and vegetables from central Florida on their way to the Gulf of Mexico.

The **Great Miami Hurricane of 1926** devastated the area. The storm surge from the lake caused widespread death and destruction. The town didn't have a chance to recover because it was hit soon after by the **1928 Okeechobee Hurricane**. That storm finished off the areas that had escaped damage in 1926 and killed thousands of people.

Moore Haven is home to the Annual **Chalo Nitka Festival and Rodeo,** which is held the first weekend in March. The first Chalo Nitka Festival was held in 1949 with LaBelle, Pahokee, Belle Glade and Moore Haven High School bands and colorful floats leading a parade down Main Street.

Chalo Nitka is Seminole for **"Big Bass."** The festival became an annual event, featuring an annual fishing tournament saluting the Black Bass. Fishing, fish camps and fishing guiding are important parts of the Moore Haven economy.

Okeechobee

Okeechobee is the county seat of Okeechobee County, the immediate area surrounding Lake Okeechobee. About 6,000 people live in Okeechobee. Some Floridians also refer to the town as **"Okeechobee City."**

It is located at the intersections of State Road 70, US-441, US-98 and County Road 710, a couple of miles north of Lake Okeechobee.

Okeechobee is the seat of government in Okeechobee County. The County courthouse was built in 1926. City Hall was built in the same year. In its early years the town was the center of the cattle industry in south Central Florida, and was also the cornerstone of Florida's freshwater fishing industry, especially **catfish** and **perch**.

Those same industries are important today, as well as tourism. People come from all over the world to enjoy fishing in Lake Okeechobee.

In the Second Seminole War, **The Battle of Lake Okeechobee** was fought between 800 troops under **Colonel Zachary Taylor**, and about half that many Seminole warriors led by **Billy Bowlegs**, **Abiaca** and **Alligator** on Christmas Day, 1837.

Both the Seminoles and Americans claimed victory, but Colonel Taylor was promoted to Brigadier General after the battle. His nickname became **"Old Rough and Ready"** after this battle, and he went on to become the **Twelfth President of the United States**.

Downtown Okeechobee is on a wide grassy boulevard with military monuments, artifacts, and shady places to sit and enjoy the view. There are plenty of shops and restaurants in town, and a couple of very nice murals and historic buildings.

THE OKEECHOBEE WATERWAY

This waterway was completed in 1937 as part of the major flood control projects that impacted the Everglades. Today it is a system of rivers, canals and locks that provide a major recreational resource to the state but also serve as a reminder of the major impact that flood control had on the natural systems.

This peaceful waterway goes through miles of untouched Florida Everglades and thousands of acres of Old Florida scrub and ranchland. It is the only navigable cross Florida canal.

Landlubbers can also enjoy the waterway at the various locks and parks along the route. It's fun to watch the boats pass through the locks along the route.

The waterway is 154 miles long and stretches from the Atlantic Ocean near Stuart, Florida to the Gulf of Mexico at Fort Myers. It is the only true cross Florida canal and river system that joins the east coast of Florida to the west coast.

The eastern reach of the waterway starts in the St. Lucie River, passes through the St Lucie lock and dam, and enters Lake Okeechobee through a lock at Port Mayaca.

From Port Mayaca you cross 451,000 acre Lake Okeechobee by either a direct route to Clewiston, or a longer route along the south edge of the lake called the "rim route."

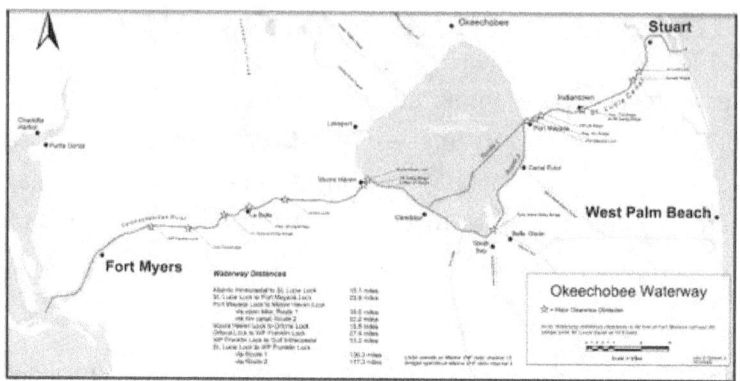

From Clewiston the waterway continues west on the Caloosahatchee River to Fort Myers. Take a look at the Okeechobee waterway map above for details of the route.

A more detailed Okeechobee waterway map with water depths, day marker, courses, bearings and other information can be purchased at West Marine or other marine stores either as a chart or a book.

Lake Okeechobee and the Okeechobee Waterway are part of the complex water management system known as the **Central and Southern Florida Flood Control Project**. This project was built by the U.S. Army Corps of Engineers (ACOE), and is managed by them and by the **South Florida Water Management District (SFWMD)**. This project covers 16,000 square miles from just south of Orlando down through the Kissimmee River to Lake Okeechobee and on south to Everglades National Park and Florida Bay in the Keys. This project is of vital importance to the Florida Everglades.

There are five locks and dams on the Okeechobee Waterway

The ACOE operates these locks and dams along the Okeechobee Waterway. From East to West they are:

St. Lucie Lock and Dam near Stuart
Port Mayaca Lock and Dam near Canal Point
Moore Haven Lock and Dam at Moore Haven
Ortona Lock and Dam east of LaBelle
Franklin Lock and Dam east of Fort Myers

Each lock location has a recreational area that is open to the public for year round use. Some of these areas have camping and picnic facilities.

This aerial view of the St Lucie Lock and Dam shows you the adjacent recreational area.

The Okeechobee Waterway was officially opened on March 23, 1937.

My Personal Trip across the Waterway

Some 67 years after the Okeechobee Waterway opened, some friends and I took a trip from east to west along the waterway in my 26 foot Island Packet sailboat, **AWOL**. Here are some highlights of that trip.

The trip began in Coconut Grove on Biscayne Bay, and after a couple of days on the Intracoastal Waterway, we spent the night at a marina in Stuart, ready for the start of the adventure.

We then headed west up the south fork of the St. Lucie River until we came to the first lock. This lock raises your boat several feet to a regulated height above sea level and that height is the controlled elevation of the St. Lucie River west of the lock.

The next three photographs are of the St. Lucie lock.

The St. Lucie Lock and Dam is the first of five such locks we encountered on the Okeechobee Waterway.

This lock is a few miles up the St Lucie River from Stuart. The sign on the rail shows you how far it is to each of the other locks.

Passing through the locks is easy; the lock tenders know their business very well and help you adjust your lines as the water level rises or lowers in the lock.

From the St. Lucie lock we continued at sailboat speed (about 6 mph) to our next stop for the night, the Indiantown Marina. This is a full service operation that specializes in boat owners who like to do their own work. They have a huge storage yard with various interesting boats that make a great experience just to stroll around and look.

There was a beautiful sunrise as we left the Indiantown marina and continued chugging westward on the quiet St Lucie Canal to **Port Mayaca** and **Lake Okeechobee**.

If you have a sailboat, you should be aware that the controlling height on the waterway is the 49' raised railway bridge at **Port Mayaca**. A mast as high as 55' can pass through, however, if the boat is heeled over by the weight of water-filled barrels tied to a sail halyard and pulled to one side of the boat. This is a service provided by a guy working out of the Indiantown Marina.

We didn't need it but it's nice to know the service is there for the bigger sailboats.

We were raised up in the Port Mayaca lock to the level of Lake Okeechobee and raised our sails for the long sail across the lake directly to Clewiston. Alas, however, our main sail halyard parted and we decided to use the engine and take the southern route along the shore of the lake.

After a day chugging along the southern shore of Lake Okeechobee (called the rim route), we came to Roland Martin's Marina in Clewiston. **Roland Martin** is a famous fishing celebrity. His little resort has motel rooms and some boat slips. A shuttle bus will come to the marina and take you to the nearby **Clewiston Inn** where you can enjoy the famously tasty Lake Okeechobee fried catfish.

Ogden Nash once wrote "A marvelous bird is the pelican, his beak can hold more than his belly can." This guy (or gal) is a fine specimen who didn't mind our presence at all. He would be in heaven if you took him to the all-you-can eat catfish dinners at the Clewiston Inn.

The dock at Roland Martin's is a very nice place to spend the night in the company of pelicans, gators and bass fishermen.

This little Gator visited us in our slip at Roland Martin's. We are smart Floridians, and knew better than to feed these guys. Do it too often and you soon become the food.

The early morning hours were abuzz with the little bass fishing boats and their crews getting ready to head out to Lake Okeechobee for a fishing tournament. The lake and its shallow shorelines are known for the best bass fishing along the Okeechobee Waterway.

We left Roland Martin's in the morning and powered slowly toward Moore Haven, the last town on Lake Okeechobee and the head of the Caloosahatchee River segment of the Waterway.

Somewhere out west of Moore Haven these horses were grazing on the kind of ranch land that Patrick Smith describes in his classic novel **"A Land Remembered."**

There was a quiet little marina at **Port LaBelle** east of the town of LaBelle where we spent a quiet night. The weather took a

February turn for the cold, so we shivered a bit and were glad to have the warmth of another human being nearby.

As of the publication of this book in 2016, this little marina at Port LaBelle is gone, replaced by a larger modern version with 100 slips and all the modern amenities.

Further west from Port LaBelle, about 2 miles west of Alva there was a quiet little marina called Rialto Harbour. It was in a secluded oxbow of the river. Natives of the Caloosahatchee

River call these oxbows **"dead river."** If you call it an oxbow they automatically know you're an outsider. An oxbow – and a dead river - is a U shaped body of water that forms when a meander from the main channel of a river gets cut off.

Rialto was a great place to spend a couple of nights. It was owned by a wonderful family. Their few employees were also like family. It was still a cold winter night, and the owners built a fire in the fire ring and cranked up the charcoal grills for a cook out and story-telling session around the fire.

I received word in 2013 that Rialto Harbour is closed for business. I wanted to cry.

Information about the Okeechobee Waterway that you should know in planning your own trip is at the U.S. Army Corps of Engineers website listed in the RESOURCES FOR FURTHER STUDY section of this book.

This little squirrel on a Rialto Harbour tree agreed with us as we sadly powered back out to the Caloosahatchee River on a cold winter morning to leave the Okeechobee Waterway. We could almost hear him say:

"Nuts! It's time to put the boat away and get back to our real jobs."

RESOURCES FOR FURTHER STUDY

This book has hopefully given you a little better understanding of the complex forces involved in the efforts involved in saving the Everglades. Here are some resources that can give you more details about the Florida Everglades.

Friends of the Everglades. This organization was founded by environmental advocate Marjory Stoneman Douglas and is well informed on all issues concerning the Everglades.
http://www.everglades.org

EvergladesRestoration.gov is the official U.S. Government website that was set up to keep interested parties informed about restoration issues and progress.
http://evergladesrestoration.gov

South Florida Water Management District. They are the successor to the old Central and South Florida Flood Control District and are co-managers with the U.S. Army Corps of Engineers of the Comprehensive Everglades Restoration Plan.
https://www.sfwmd.gov/

U.S. Army Corps of Engineers. They are co-managers with the SFWMD and maintain a status of all ongoing projects of the Comprehensive Everglades Restoration Plan.
http://www.saj.usace.army.mil/Missions/Environmental/Ecosystem-Restoration/

Okeechobee Waterway. This is an Army website with current conditions on the waterway.
http://www.saj.usace.army.mil/Missions/Civil-Works/Lake-Okeechobee/Okeechobee-Waterway-OWW/

Seminole Tribe. Their official website tells you about their history and current activities.
http://seminoletribe.com/

Totch: A Life in the Everglades is available at Amazon.com. Totch Brown was an Everglades legend who made his living in the Chokoloskee and Everglades City area. His life and others have been impacted by things that have happened to the Everglades in modern times.

The 1928 Hurricane and Its Impact. This is a Wikipedia article that describes the killer storm and its impact on the people in the area and in the nation's attitude about flood control.
https://en.wikipedia.org/wiki/1928_Okeechobee_hurricane

The Swamp: The Everglades, Florida, and the Politics of Paradise. is available at Amazon.com. This book by Michael Grunwald gives a highly detailed account of what happened to the Everglades and what is happening now.

River of Grass is available at Amazon.com. This old classic by Marjory Stoneman Douglas was written in 1947 and is credited by many with starting the awareness of the Everglades leading to the formation of Everglades National Park and the modern movements to save the Everglades.

Big Cypress Loop Road and Lucky's Place. This is a residence and photographer's studio south of Tamiami Trail in the heart of the Everglades. The link is to a website page about the road and Lucky's.
http://www.florida-backroads-travel.com/big-cypress-loop-road.html

Florida Everglades Things to Do. Links to a variety of places and attractions you can enjoy.
http://www.florida-everglades.com/active.htm

EPILOGUE

Mike Miller has lived in Florida since 1960. He graduated from the University of Florida with a degree in civil engineering and has lived and worked in most areas of Florida. His projects include Walt Disney World, EPCOT, Universal Studios and hundreds of commercial, municipal and residential developments all over the state including engineering work for the South Florida Water Management District related to the Comprehensive Everglades Restoration Plan.

During that time, Mike developed an understanding and love of Old Florida that is reflected in the pages of his website, **Florida-Backroads-Travel.com**. The website contains several hundred pages about places in Florida and things to do. The information on the website is organized into the eight geographical regions of the state and the Florida Everglades.

This book - **Florida Everglades** - is based on the website. It can be purchased at Amazon in either Kindle or soft cover format.

If you find any inaccuracies in this guide, including restaurants or attractions that have closed, please contact Mike at Florida-Backroads-Travel.com and let him know. It is his intention to update the guide periodically and publish updated editions.

If you have enjoyed this book and purchased it at Amazon or any other bookstore, Mike would appreciate it if you would take a couple of minutes to post a short review at Amazon. Thoughtful reviews help other customers make better buying choices. He reads all of his reviews personally, and each one helps him write better books in the future. Thanks for your support!

BOOKS BY MIKE MILLER

Florida Backroads Travel
Northwest Florida Backroads Travel
North Central Florida Backroads Travel
Northeast Florida Backraods Travel
Central East Florida Backroads Travel
Central Florida Backroads Travel
Central West Florida Backroads Travel
Southwest Florida Backroads Travel
Southeast Florida Backroads Travel
Florida Everglades
Florida Wineries
Florida Festivals
Florida Carpenter Gothic Churches
Florida One Tank Trips, Volume 1
Florida Heritage Travel, Volumes I, II, III
Living Aboard a Boat
Florida Wineries
What Would Walt Do?

www.ingramcontent.com/pod-product-compliance
Lightning Source LLC
Chambersburg PA
CBHW060228290526
45789CB00003B/1466